T0299653

Building Confidence, Resilience and Emotional Intelligence in Young Children

of related interest

Provocations for Learning in Early Years Settings
A Practical Guide
Margaret Longstaffe
ISBN 978 1 78592 495 8
eISBN 978 1 78450 882 1

Self-Regulation Skills in Young Children
Activities and Strategies for Practitioners and Parents
Sue Asquith
ISBN 978 1 78775 196 5
eISBN 978 1 78775 197 2

Exercising Muscles and Minds, Second Edition
Outdoor Play and the Early Years Curriculum
Marjorie Ouvry and Amanda Furtado
ISBN 978 1 78592 266 4
eISBN 978 1 78450 557 8

The Early Years Movement Handbook
A Principles-Based Approach to Supporting Young Children's
Physical Development, Health and Wellbeing
Lala Manners
Illustrated by Tilly Power
Foreword by Professor Gareth Stratton
ISBN 978 1 78592 260 2
eISBN 978 1 78450 546 2

Forest School and Autism
A Practical Guide
Michael James
ISBN 978 1 78592 291 6
eISBN 978 1 78450 595 0

Nurturing Personal, Social and Emotional
Development in Early Childhood
A Practical Guide to Understanding Brain Development
and Young Children's Behaviour
Debbie Garvey
Foreword by Dr Suzanne Zeedyk
ISBN 978 1 78592 223 7
eISBN 978 1 78450 500 4

Building Confidence, Resilience and Emotional Intelligence in Young Children

A Practical Guide Using Growth Mindset, Forest School and Multiple Intelligences

Jamie Victoria Barnes

Jessica Kingsley Publishers
London and Philadelphia

First published in 2020
by Jessica Kingsley Publishers
73 Collier Street
London N1 9BE, UK
and
400 Market Street, Suite 400
Philadelphia, PA 19106, USA

www.jkp.com

Library of Congress Cataloging in Publication Data
A CIP catalog record for this book is available from the Library of Congress

British Library Cataloguing in Publication Data
A CIP catalogue record for this book is available from the British Library

ISBN 978 1 78775 160 6
eISBN 978 1 78775 161 3

Printed and bound in Great Britain

For my loving and supportive grandparents: Kath, Ada, Gordon and Les. Grandad Les, you always told me, 'You can do whatever you want, sweetheart', so I did. Your grit and determination in all that you do, and your love of books inspires me no end. I hope this one you enjoy the most.

Contents

Acknowledgements

When you step out of your comfort zone you find yourself in a place where the magic happens. I stepped out of my comfort zone, made myself known and was given the opportunity to write my first book. This is something I have always dreamt of doing. It has not been an easy task but it has been unbelievably rewarding.

There are many people I would like to thank for helping with this book, people who have believed in me, inspired me and supported me. Thank you to the incredible professors such as Howard Gardner and Carol Dweck, who have inspired this book, and to the truly amazing children I have had the opportunity to work with over the years.

I wouldn't be where I am today without my parents, who have been my cheerleaders from day one. Thank you for always building my confidence, guiding me and making me believe that anything is possible. Thank you from the bottom of my heart.

To my friends and sister who have all put up with my constant talk about this book and the endless questions and queries – I am incredibly lucky to have you all in my life, thank you.

To my husband for putting up with my long evenings and weekends of work! You have always encouraged me to follow my dreams and have never doubted me for a minute. Thank you for all of your support. Always.

Lastly, to everyone at JKP for their help and guidance in putting this book together. I have learned so much along the way, including how long I thought it would take to write a book, and how long it actually takes! Special thanks to Jane, my editor, for believing in my idea and giving me the opportunity to publish my first book – I can't tell you how grateful I am.

Introduction

Pamela Stevens was a primary school teacher in England who dedicated her life to teaching and mentoring hundreds of young children. She saw something in every child who walked into her classroom and knew that each child was gifted in their own way. Pamela gave all of her students the support and guidance they needed to flourish, whether at school or as a tutor in her spare time. Pamela knew that teaching certainly was not a 'one-size-fits-all' method and that she had to work her magic to support each style of learner in her class, giving them the confidence in their own abilities to shine and develop.

It is not every day that you come across a teacher like Pamela, and I was fortunate to be one of her students; aged seven, I stepped into her classroom midway through the year and academically behind in comparison with the rest of the class. Pamela was supportive and nurturing and never tolerated any nonsense; I can remember saying on many occasions, 'I can't do it' and she would turn to look at me and say, 'Of course you can do it, now let's get on.' There was never any doubt in her mind that I couldn't achieve, and she displayed it in a way that I understood. Pamela, or Mrs Stevens as I knew her then, went on to tutor me every Saturday morning for some time to support me with English and maths during my later primary years, and we kept in touch until she sadly passed away in March 2014. It was overwhelming to see so many of her past students at her funeral because of the confidence, resilience and emotional support she provided to each and every one of us. Mrs Stevens gave us the ability to believe in ourselves and our talents and knew that if we put our minds to it we could achieve anything that we wanted, and for that I will be eternally grateful. I know that she would be so proud of everything her students have gone on to achieve and if I told her I was writing a book she would have said, 'Well of course you are, Jamie', and secretly I know she would have been beaming with pride.

I think we can all look back on our lives and find someone who inspired us, who supported and gave us confidence, whether it was a teacher, a family member or a friend. The impact that somebody can have on our life, both positive and negative, can shape our journeys, especially in our early years when 90 per cent of brain development occurs by the age of five years and our experiences during this time have a profound impact on our future.

I wanted to create a book that enables you as the educator to understand how to support children with their confidence and self-belief, teach them how to be resilient and keep on trying even when something is tough, and allow them to be in touch with and understand their emotions. Most importantly, I want this book to be relatable, have meaning and be easy to read, because when we connect with something it is far easier to grasp it and then put it into practice.

I will be looking closely at several theories and approaches among each of the chapters, including growth mindset, Forest School and multiple intelligences. Don't worry, I am going to break them down, connect them to early years and give activity examples of how you can bring the ideas into teaching and play. When I began planning this book, I chose the content based on the fact that the theories and approaches overlap with each other and interconnect, creating a unique outlook on education.

I want you to be the educator that children look back on in the future and say, 'it was you who made an impact on my life', 'it was you who inspired and gave me confidence'. So let me help you find your confidence and self-belief in your abilities to quite literally change the lives of the young children that you teach. Author William A. Ward once said that, 'The mediocre teacher tells. The good teacher explains. The superior teacher demonstrates. The great teacher inspires' (Mertz 2010, p.118). I truly believe that incredible teachers explain, demonstrate and inspire their children, but those who build their confidence and believe in their children too, are second to none.

CHAPTER 1

The Multiple Intelligence Approach to Early Years

If you take a look at your friendship group, your family or work colleagues, you will notice that everyone is completely different, no one person is the same. Indeed, that sounds rather obvious, but when you really notice how unique each individual is you begin to stop comparing yourself and start to appreciate your personal strengths and others. For example, my group of friends could not be a more diverse group; we all attended the same school, lived in the same area and had fairly similar upbringings, yet we have all have totally different strengths and weaknesses. For instance, one has a career in data science and another in high-end fashion – both have very different careers and both are very successful and talented. What I am trying to say is that the world would be a very boring place if everyone was good at the same thing, there is a place for all talents and aptitudes – we all have multiple intelligences.

This chapter is all about multiple intelligences. What does that mean, I hear you ask. Well let me enlighten you… I came across this approach when I took on a role as deputy head teacher at a multiple intelligence school in Surrey, England. The school's curriculum was based around this theory and aimed to support children's emotional, social and academic intelligences – all children were recognized for their uniqueness and individual talents. Howard Gardner, an American psychologist, designed the 'multiple intelligence (MI) theory'. The theory looks to show that everyone has an intelligence and no person is the same, so why would we expect everyone to learn and understand in the same way as each other? The MI theory gives empowerment to each individual, as everyone is valued and no type of intelligence is given more importance than another, leaving them all having an equal status.

To give an example, if a child's talents are art and dance they should not be thought of as any lesser than a child whose talents are mathematics and science. Society has always put far more emphasis on the importance of maths, literacy and science than it has on any other learning area or subject, especially when children go through primary and secondary school, which has meant that a lot of children then feel inferior if their particular talent or strength does not come under those three categories. Don't get me wrong, in a child's early years, mathematics and literacy are hugely important areas for development and learning but it doesn't mean that if they struggle with these areas they are not intelligent – it may mean that their strengths lie elsewhere or perhaps they need to be taught in a different way. This quote from cartoonist George Evans sums this up nicely, 'Every student can learn, just not on the same day or in the same way' (Litchka 2019, p.x).

Being an educator or parent you can find that some days you have mastered your teaching and the children understand and thrive, and the next day the same method simply does not work. First, this is totally normal, and second, children are ever changing, growing and developing, so it is the supreme art of the teacher to engage and connect with their children and teach with fluidity and flexibility.

The MI approach struck a chord with me straightaway because I instantly identified with that child who felt inferior at school, especially as I reached secondary school. Mathematics and I have never got on…it just did not 'click' with me and I struggled with science too and was put in the bottom sets for both, which does nothing for your self-esteem! I found English easier and I especially enjoyed creative writing; drama was my strong point but sadly that was not given as much importance as science and maths. I felt as though I had been boxed or categorized as less intelligent, when really I was intelligent all along, just not in the subjects that the school deemed most important. Luckily, my family have always been hugely supportive of my achievements and strengths and have always encouraged me to pursue my dreams. I would not be where I am today without them. It is far easier for us to build up children and instil a sense of self-worth and confidence than try to convince an adult in later life that they can achieve and be successful when they have not been supported and guided in their early years.

The eight intelligences

Howard Gardner (1993) believes that intelligence can be split into eight areas: verbal, logical, kinaesthetic, rhythmic, inter-personal, intra-personal, visual and naturalist, the latter having been added at a later date to the original seven. A person can fall under one or more of these eight areas but an outlying strength will usually be visible.

I personally find diagrams and visual cues hugely beneficial so for those of you who are visual learners like me, here is a diagram to showcase those eight intelligences.

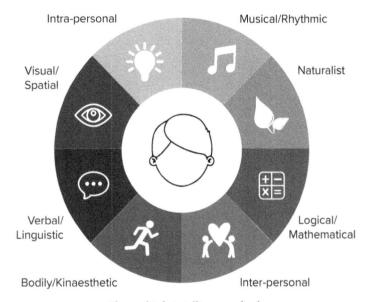

The multiple intelligence wheel

Now let me explain each of these intelligences in more detail as initially it took me a while to get my head around it, so I want to support you in understanding it as best as I can.

Intra-personal intelligence

First, intra means 'within', so this intelligence is all about connecting with your inner feelings and emotions. People with this intelligence are often independent and have great self-awareness; they like to reflect on themselves and analyze situations, feelings, relationships and emotions.

How does a young child show this intelligence?

- They have good self-awareness.

- They often like working independently.

- They are able to regulate their emotions and feelings.

- They like to analyze and work something out in an order or method.

- They understand and talk about emotions and feelings and how they can affect others.

What roles might they be good at as an adult?

- writer

- philosopher

- scientist

- engineer

- psychologist.

Inter-personal intelligence

This intelligence is about relationships and communication with others. Those with this intelligence are great at under-standing others, communicating and interacting while picking up on emotional and social cues. A 'people person' is often a term used to describe those who are sociable around others and it fits in well with this intelligence.

How does a young child show this intelligence?

- They are a good communicator (verbally and non-verbally).

- They are sociable with others.

- They are good at relating to and understanding others' emotions.

- They work well in a group and are a team player.

What roles might they be good at as an adult?

- salesperson

- manager

- politician

- teacher

- counsellor

- public relations.

Musical intelligence

This intelligence speaks for itself – musical and rhythmic. Someone with this intelligence is good at learning songs and melodies, enjoys singing or playing musical instruments and has good rhythm.

How does a young child show this intelligence?

- They enjoy songs/music/sound.

- They like to sing.

- They have good rhythm.

- They explore musical instruments.

- They create their own sounds/rhythms.

What roles might they be good at as an adult?

- musician

- singer

- songwriter

- composer

- conductor

- music teacher.

Bodily/Kinaesthetic intelligence

Kinaesthetic means being aware of your body and how to move it. Those with this intelligence learn through movement and doing. They typically have excellent gross and fine motor skills and enjoy physical activities. They like to figure out how to do something, and take a hands-on approach to learning.

How does a young child show this intelligence?

- They are excellent at moving.

- They have good gross and fine motor skills.

- They enjoy learning through a hands-on approach.

- They are energetic and active.

- They enjoy the outdoors and sports.

- They like crafts.

What roles might they be good at as an adult?

- dancer

- actor/actress

- athlete/sports person

- carpenter

- construction worker.

Logical/Mathematical intelligence

Those with this intelligence are excellent problem solvers who enjoy numbers, patterns and analyzing. Working with numbers comes naturally and they work with logic and reason.

How does a young child show this intelligence?

- They enjoy puzzles.

- They like counting.

- They group objects.

- They create patterns and problem solve.

What roles might they be good at as an adult?

- mathematician

- data scientist

- scientist

- maths teacher

- accountant

- computer programmer

- medical doctor.

Linguistic intelligence

This involves the ability to use words well both when writing and speaking. They enjoy reading and writing, and often pick up different languages easily. They learn new words and have a large vocabulary; they excel at communicating through written tasks.

How does a young child show this intelligence?

- They enjoy stories.

- They show an interest in letters, sounds and words.

- They communicate very well.

- They enjoy mark making and writing.

- They create their own stories.

- They enjoy learning new languages.

What roles might they be good at as an adult?

- writer

- journalist

- copywriter

- linguist

- translator

- editor.

Visual/Spatial intelligence

This intelligence is for those who are good at being aware of their surroundings and naturally have a good sense of direction. They are also excellent with remembering images, places and patterns, often with vivid imagination which they can create into visual images. They are also very good with colours, shapes and space.

How does a young child show this intelligence?

- They like to paint and draw.

- They explore craft activities.

- They are interested in colours.

- They have good spatial awareness.

- They have good fine motor control.

- They notice finer details in their environment.

What roles might they be good at as an adult?

- artist

- graphic designer

- architect

- photographer

- fashion designer

- engineer.

Naturalist intelligence

This intelligence was created after the first seven when Gardner originally came up with his theory. Those with this intelligence have a strong connection with nature and the outdoor environment; they notice their surroundings and the changes that take place. Wildlife and plants, trees and anything based around nature are of great interest.

How does a young child show this intelligence?

- They have a love for the outdoors.

- They notice their environment and the changes that occur.

- They explore confidently outside.

- They enjoy planting and gardening.

- They are inquisitive about the world around them.

- They show interest in wildlife and animals.

What roles might they be good at as an adult?

- farmer

- gardener

- conservationist

- landscaper

- vet

- biologist

- Forest School teacher.

These are the eight intelligences, and each person will show strengths in more than one of them. When we can identify someone's intelligences it makes teaching so much easier because we understand how that person learns. For example, a person who is very active and learns through a hands-on approach (bodily/kinaesthetic intelligence) will not understand mathematics unless they can use tactile resources and move their body while learning. A perfect activity for them would be to search for hidden objects in a garden area and, once these are collected, count out the objects and place the correct amount onto a given number card. This way they are able to move about using their energy and make connections with the activity in a way that suits their learning style.

As educators, we have to be creative in our methods to teach and support each type of learner to bring out the best of their abilities. The world is diverse and it is vital that we realize this and understand that therefore education must also be diverse and fluid. In an interview in 1997, Howard Gardner (Edutopia 2008) said:

Education which treats everyone the same way is actually the most unfair education because it picks out one kind of mind and if you think like that, great, but if you don't then there is no room on the train for you.

I think a lot of people will be able to relate to this. How often were your talents overlooked because they did not fit society's ideal mould of what 'intelligence' or 'success' was? If you are that learner who fits the way mainstream education is taught, then great! But what about the rest of us? When are educators, leaders and governors going to realize that because we are all different, we learn differently too? It is crucial that we understand how to teach fluidly and give information in a variety of means so that everybody has the chance to learn and, more importantly, understand.

If we know that one child has a very spatial or visual way of learning, another child has a very hands-on way of learning and a third child likes stories, we do not have to talk very fast as a teacher; we can provide software, materials and resources which present material to a child in a way in which the child will find interesting so they can use their intelligences productively and show their understanding in a way that is comfortable to that child. (Edutopia 2008)

We have been programmed to see intelligence in a certain way, or we categorize a type of person to fit that criteria. What we need to do is shift out mindset to realize that intelligence comes in many forms and as educators we can tailor our teaching to suit all intelligences.

As you know, a child's early years are crucial in laying the foundations for later development, growth and success. Whether you work in a nursery, a preschool, as a childminder or nanny, your influences will have a great impact on the children you look after. It is imperative that we instil confidence in each child's abilities, which is what the MI approach looks to achieve. Children should be celebrated!

Positivity, support and belief in young children and their abilities are fundamental in building their self-confidence. As early educators, we can use the MI theory in our everyday practices with the young children we teach and care for. If a child is not understanding in a way that we are teaching, then rather than believing the child can't do the task, we should reflect on the way we are teaching and think about what we can do to modify and change our methods, not the child. This way, we can also learn how to be effective educators who cater for each child's individual needs and qualities, as well as improve and grow ourselves.

Supporting each learner

I will now share with you how you can take a simple activity and deliver it to all types of learner individually, following the MI theory.

You have decided to teach your children about the weather and seasons; some of the children may pick it up immediately and others may take longer to grasp the concept. This is not only completely normal but also a reflection that not all children learn and understand in the same way. So, as an example, here are some ideas as to what you can use to support children who fall under one of more of the eight intelligences when teaching about the weather and seasons:

- *Intra-personal/Introspective:* a story or picture book relating to that child personally

- *Inter-personal/Social:* a group activity, such as a turn-taking card game

- *Musical/Rhythmic:* a song, rhyme or poem

- *Bodily/Kinaesthetic:* an active game, involving movement

- *Logical/Mathematical:* a puzzle

- *Verbal/Linguistic:* a story book or audio tape

- *Visual/Spatial:* a calendar visual aid

- *Naturalist:* outdoor, hands-on experience.

I appreciate that when we teach large groups of children it is not always possible to tailor every aspect to each individual, which is why I suggest you create activities and sessions that take a holistic approach to learning and development. The word holistic means 'whole' and in terms of children and teaching it would aim to focus on the whole child – not just their academic learning, but all aspects of their learning and development, including their social, emotional and physical development too. The Early Years Foundation Stage (EYFS) is the statutory guidance that all early years providers in England must legally follow. Within the EYFS there are seven areas of learning. Here is how a child's multiple intelligences can fit into these seven learning areas:

- personal, social and emotional (inter-personal and intra-personal)

- communication and language (linguistic and inter-personal)

- physical (bodily/kinaesthetic and spatial/visual)

- literacy (linguistic)

- mathematics (logical/mathematical)

- understanding of the world (naturalist, visual/spatial and bodily/kinaesthetic)

- expressive arts and design (musical and visual/spatial).

When I plan activities with young children, I take the holistic approach and create sessions that aim to support all or most of these seven areas. Regardless of whether you are based in England or another country, you can apply this idea to the framework you follow. A holistic session provides children with rich opportunities for learning and developing as well as supporting their multiple intelligences. Here is an activity plan example that you can follow:

ACTIVITY: Using our five senses

Activity aims:

- Encourage awareness of our five senses and how we use them. The activity allows the children to act out the story, so they can become fully involved in understanding and interpreting the book. It allows creativity, imagination and communication between each other.

Main activity:

- Introduce the five senses, encouraging the children to act out scenarios. For example, 'taste' – how would you react if you ate a lemon? Or 'touch' – how would you react if you touched an ice cube?

- Read a story to the children (*The Gruffalo* by Julia Donaldson, 1999). Then take the children on an adventure in the outdoor area to act out the story, making particular reference to all the senses used. Introduce the activity by saying something like: 'Let's collect items to represent each animal from the story on our travels through the woods. Use your senses to spot any animal homes.'

- Reflect as a group on what senses were used when acting out the story together. Refer to the pictures in the book and discuss facial expressions, feelings/emotions and body language. For example, 'How do you think the Owl felt when he heard about a Gruffalo?'

The session supports:

- personal, social and emotional development (teamwork, communication and discussion of emotions)

- communication and language (speaking, voicing ideas, conversation and listening skills)

- physical (outdoor play, five senses, movement)

- expressive arts and design (imaginative role play)

- understanding of the world (being in the natural world and using its resources, looking out for wildlife and their habitats)

- mathematics (sequence of events within the story, collecting and counting items to represent animals during the story)

- literacy (storytelling).

When you begin planning activities and try to incorporate all areas of a child's learning and development, you will soon pick up how much more involved and responsive the children are to this way of teaching, and how it gives them greater opportunities. Children flourish when they feel that they can achieve, and by planning holistic activities we can support all types of learner and give them the platform they need to succeed.

Supporting the individual

Early childhood passes us by quickly and the rate of development and growth is vast in such a short space of time, which means we have to make the most of it and allow children to enjoy being children and to learn through play and exploration. Combining this thinking and the MI approach, we can certainly create an environment for young children that gives them the best possible start to life and cements those foundations in place so that they continue to succeed as they grow older. Confidence comes from within, as long as the child has had someone supporting, praising and believing in them from the start. As soon as they are made to feel inferior or less important because their intelligences do not fit with the stereotype of mainstream education, confidence is lost and child begins to doubt and question what they are truly good at. Positivity is essential, and an open mindset to reflect and be the best educator we can be is the recipe for being an effective teacher.

Now, it is not only important for us to recognize that every child has a talent and strength but also that we do as educators. Find out where your intelligences lie, celebrate your strengths and use them to inspire your children! For example, I love to be creative and imaginative so I use those strengths when coming up with activity and play ideas – the children bounce off of your energy because you are excited about what you want to deliver! It also helps us strengthen our work as a team and give each other platforms for our talents as teachers. Just like your friendship group, your work colleagues will all have different strengths and weaknesses too, and together that can create a powerful team with members who balance each other out.

I often deliver training to staff teams and one moment during a training session will stay with me always. The purpose of this particular session was to inspire the staff, support them with creative activity ideas and encourage them to see their outdoor area in a new light. The nursery, based in London, had a wonderful staff team who worked really well together, but I wanted them to understand about their own strengths so they could be the best educators that they could be. During the afternoon, we were in the outdoor area and I had asked them to gather resources so I could teach them how to make natural picture frames that they could then weave and decorate.

The team quite literally spent ages doing this; they were engrossed in making their frames, choosing their wool to weave and gathering natural resources to decorate and create a unique picture. It was January and freezing cold, but none of them minded because they were having such fun (which is what I say about children – they are not fazed by the weather as long as they have appropriate clothing and engaging play). At the end of the training day, one of the members of staff came up to me, hugged me and started to cry. Alarmed I asked if she was ok, to which she responded:

> I moved to England from the Philippines so many years ago, and my spoken English is good but I have always focused on the fact that my written English is not as good as everyone else's, and today you made me realize what my strengths and talents are. Sat outside making the picture frames reminded me of my childhood in the Philippines, where we would spend hours making toys and games and I remembered just how good I am at crafts and being creative. I don't need to worry about my written English and I need to focus on what I am good at, so thank you so much.

I shed a tear or two on my drive home because I am so glad that she realized her strengths and will no longer focus solely on her weaknesses; she found her intelligence and that realization was overwhelming. I am so grateful that I was able to be a part of that moment – it truly meant a lot.

Remember – intelligence is so much more than the ability to answer questions in a test. We all learn, but in different ways.

We are all intelligent in a multitude of ways.

Reflection

After each chapter, we will reflect on the themes discussed through a series of questions that will enable you to reflect on yourself and your children. When we reflect we can understand how and why certain events went well and why some did not. Reflection is an opportunity to support yourself and your children to the highest level, ensuring development. I recommend creating a self-reflection scrapbook or diary, with the aim for this to be a working document that you update and review regularly. Each chapter in this book will look at different reflective questions, which you can take and use to answer questions about yourself and your children. To be effective we must be reflective!

Self-reflection

1. What were your strengths and weaknesses as a child?

2. What are your strengths and weaknesses as an adult?

3. How did your strengths and weaknesses make you feel as a child and how do they make you feel now?

4. Can you see a range of different intelligences among your friends and family?

5. What type of learner are you?

6. What are your multiple intelligences?

7. What was your education like? Write down the positives and negatives.

8. If you could give your child self a message, what would it be?

Teaching reflection

1. Look at the children in your class or group. What are their individual strengths and weaknesses?

2. Can you work out their multiple intelligences?

3. How can you use this knowledge to tailor your teaching to suit their needs?

4. Reflect on a time where an activity or lesson you taught worked really well. Why do you think this was?

5. Reflect on a time where an activity or lesson you taught did not go to plan. Why do you think this was?

6. What have you learned from your reflections that you can take forward?

CHAPTER 2

Building Confident and Resilient Children

What is resilience?

I will never forget when I watched Bertie climb to the top of a slippery muddy bank in the woods where we had stopped to play; the smile on his face was truly magnificent. Bertie had just turned four years and attended the Forest School nursery that I was managing at the time. Bertie had been attempting to climb this bank for a few weeks and although he would get part way up, he kept sliding back down. I stood by and watched, giving words of encouragement, 'Keep on trying, Bertie! You are doing really well!' and as it was time to move on, 'Don't worry, Bertie, we will be back tomorrow and you can try again.' I knew that this was something Bertie needed to figure out and master by himself, because if I gave him all the answers on how to climb this bank, all I would really be teaching him was that I was better at navigating and working it out than he was. I offered a few strategy ideas and open-ended questions such as, 'Is there anything you could use to help you get to the top?' just to get him thinking. What I did know was that every time Bertie failed in climbing the bank, he was learning, making connections and figuring out his next move. As I stood by each time, encouraging him when he slid down the bank again and reassuring him that he could do it, he didn't give up. Yes, understandably he did throw a slight tantrum one day when he was so close to reaching his goal, but I sat with him and asked him how he felt, and he was upset that he couldn't climb like James could. Again, I provided the reassurance that he would do it but he just had to keep trying and not give up – we only don't succeed if we stop trying. With this in mind, Bertie kept on trying; his perseverance was incredible and on many occasions it was so tempting for me to just give him all the answers to his problem but I knew with the odd hint or new strategy from me to support him, he would master it.

The day finally came when Bertie had learned from all the previous mistakes he had made when climbing the bank, his physical strength had improved and his determination was stronger than ever – he reached the top! At first he said nothing. I think even he was in disbelief that after weeks of trying he had actually managed it. 'Jamie, Jamie, I did it! I did it! I'm the king of the woods!' he shouted. He was so proud of himself, he had completed what he had set out to achieve and he did that by himself through trial and error, persistence and resilience. I, the educator, supported and encouraged him along the way, giving him the confidence to believe in himself because I believed he could.

Resilience is the ability to recover from difficulties and bounce back. Bertie kept facing barriers and knock backs when trying to climb the bank, but he didn't give up – he was resilient. This is a skill all children need to be taught in their early years, so that when they do come across a problem, they try to tackle it rather than give up. Can you think of a time when you have had to be resilient? When you do achieve what you set out to do, especially when the journey has been longer and harder than you expected, the sense of achievement is so much greater...and you have learned so much along the way too. I live by this motto: FAIL = First Attempt In Learning. We never really fail at anything, because we always learn from our mistakes and know how we would do it differently next time in order to achieve what we set out to do.

The growth mindset theory

Growth mindset is a term you may have heard of, and if not, no problem because I am about to tell you all about it! Dr Carol Dweck, an American psychologist, became interested in how students reacted to failure. Dweck and her team (2012) studied thousands of children and this led to her developing the mindset theory, which is the belief that everyone either has a fixed or growth mindset.

A fixed mindset is when you believe that your intelligence or talents alone can create success. A person with a fixed mindset does not believe that they need to develop or grow their intelligences as they see them as a fixed trait. So an example would be, 'I am good at singing and I don't need to practise or train to get any better.' People with this view are often not receptive to constructive feedback, they do not ask questions to further their knowledge, they may give up easily if something is difficult and often are threatened by someone else's success. In comparison, a person with a growth mindset believes that they can develop their abilities through hard work and dedication, and they love to learn because it means they are developing resilience and continuously improving. When you have a growth mindset you embrace challenges, take on board constructive criticism, ask questions, keep on trying regardless of setbacks and are inspired by the work and success of others. As educators or parents, teaching our children to have a growth mindset from a young age will support them in building their own confidence. If we simply praise their talent, when something does go wrong they will doubt their abilities because they have not been taught to embrace challenges and hurdles. Carol Dweck (2016, pp.179–180) rightly says:

> If parents want to give their children a gift, the best thing they can do is to teach their children to love challenges, be intrigued by mistakes, enjoy effort, and keep on learning. That way, their children don't have to be slaves of praise. They will have a lifelong way to build and repair their own confidence.

Challenges, hardship and mistakes are vital ingredients for developing hard-working and successful learners.

Supporting growth mindset

As educators, we have the opportunity to instil growth mindset traits in all our children from their early years. We need to provide them with challenge so that they can test out their own abilities and work out how to problem solve and enjoy overcoming hardships because each time they do, their confidence builds too. There are three characteristics of effective teaching and learning that children should demonstrate:

- Playing and exploring – children investigate and experience things, and 'have a go'.

- Active learning – children concentrate and keep on trying if they encounter difficulties, and enjoy achievements.

- Creating and thinking critically – children have and develop their own ideas, make links between ideas and develop strategies for doing things. (Department for Education 2017)

These three characteristics are exactly what a child who has a growth mindset, excellent self-confidence and resilience would display. If we as educators are giving children a high level of quality teaching then the children we care and look after will be showing these character traits. The EYFS talks about offering children an 'enabling environment', but it does not specify exactly what this should look like as we can interpret it in our own way – there is not a preferred style. If the environment is rich with learning opportunities and the teachers are armed with knowledge on how to challenge and extend children's learning as well as to care, support and nurture them, then the children will feel safe and secure to explore and try new things out. They will be able to keep on trying when faced with a challenging activity because their teachers are there offering support when needed, which will then encourage those children to think critically and make links and ideas about how they will achieve something that is challenging.

I have put together a list of words and phrases that are very helpful in supporting children to develop a growth mindset. Try using some of these phrases when a child faces a problem:

'I can't do this.'	'You can do it. Let's try a new way.'
'It's too hard.'	'It is supposed to be hard but when we practise we get better at something.'
'I give up.'	'Let me give you some ideas on how you can move forward.'
'I did it wrong.'	'How did you get it wrong? Let's work out what we can do differently next time.'
'I'm not smart enough.'	'Being smart comes from working hard and trying. Let me give you some ideas to help.'
'I'm not good at this.'	'Nobody is good at something at the beginning; we have to keep trying to get better at something.'

If children feel as if they can't achieve something and we the adults simply say, 'Never mind, let's do something else' then we have reinforced the idea in their minds that they were not able to achieve it or they were not good enough. I understand that as a society we are always busy and rushing on to the next thing, whatever that might be. Let me give you a scenario where you could either support a growth mindset or reinforce a fixed mindset. This scenario is one I have seen plenty of times at a nursery/preschool setting but one I have seen in home environments too:

It's 11.30am at your nursery and little Rosie is struggling with a 20-piece puzzle. You can see the glum look on her face as she tries to place another puzzle piece down but it does not fit. Rosie puts the piece down and huffs, 'I can't do it', folding her arms and frowning.

What do you do? You know that in a few minutes it will be time to tidy away and get ready for lunchtime as your manager is strict on staff and children keeping to the daily routine. But in this moment, what is more important: helping Rosie finish this puzzle or telling her to try another time?

Fixed mindset approach: You go over to Rosie and she repeats to you again, 'I can't do it.' You respond with, 'Never mind, Rosie, it is tidy up time now so let's put it away and we can try another puzzle after lunch.' Rosie then reluctantly puts away her efforts in the toy box along with the puzzle pieces and follows the other children with the routine. You can see she looks sad and another staff member asks, 'What is wrong with Rosie?' You reply, 'Oh she is just a bit sad because we didn't have time to finish her puzzle as its tidy up time; she was finding it too hard anyway.'

Growth mindset approach: You go over to Rosie and she repeats to you again, 'I can't do it.' You respond with, 'I can see you have been trying really hard to put this puzzle together. Why is it not working?' Rosie looks up at you and says, 'It doesn't fit when I put it there.' This is where you realize that Rosie is not turning the puzzle pieces around to try different fits. 'Well I think that you can do it; trying something new can be hard to begin with because we need to learn how to do it first. Can I help you with an idea so you can try and finish this puzzle yourself?'

You explain and demonstrate to Rosie how to turn the puzzle pieces to see if they fit in different directions. Rosie then tries this method and realizes that sometimes that does work. Rosie puts a few more pieces together and is feeling happy and confident that she has made progress. You explain to Rosie that we have to get ready for lunch, so let's put the puzzle to one side and she can carry on her great efforts after she has eaten. Rosie is beaming with pride that she has started to figure out the puzzle and has learned a new strategy, rather than giving up and putting it away. Rosie happily goes to help tidy up as she knows she can finish the rest after lunchtime.

Now these scenarios are 'picture perfect' and you and I know that working with children does not always go so smoothly! However, I think they give a good idea of how you can support those growth mindsets from a young age. I know that we get busy and sometimes the easier option is to move on or put an activity away and try again another time, but the learning and confidence given to that child is so much greater when we support them in that moment. It could be that the extra five minutes you spend on that crucial moment is the most important part of learning they may have all day.

Entrepreneur Richard Branson said, 'You don't learn to walk by following rules. You learn by doing, and by falling over' (Smart 2017, p.149). This sticks in my mind, because it always feels as if when we are little, making mistakes is inevitable but there seems to be stigma as we get older if we don't master something straightaway. In fact, making mistakes is all part of the journey, no matter what our age, and we need to appreciate mistakes and not see them as something 'bad' but a pivotal part of our journey.

Teaching children to have that growth mindset and resilience when something doesn't go right builds their self-confidence. Another trait which I feel is hugely important is 'grit' – the determination to persevere at something. Psychologist Angela Duckworth (2007, p.1087) defines grit as 'perseverance and passion for long-term goals' – those who have grit are able to inspire themselves, have courage and fire that passion in their belly to keep motivated. Bertie had grit and determination when he was aiming to climb the bank!

It is important to remember that when children go to an early years setting or when they move on to school, you could be that one adult in their lives who is building their confidence and self-belief. As educators, we need to remind all children that they are capable of achieving and that opportunities can be accessed; we need to close the gap so that everyone has the chance to develop the knowledge and skills needed for future success.

Cultural capital

Cultural capital is about the essential knowledge that all children need to learn in order to achieve future success – the more we can understand the more we are able to do. Howard Gardner said:

> I want my children to understand the world, but not just because the world is fascinating and the human mind is curious. I want them to understand it so that they will be positioned to make it a better place. (Gardner in Illeris 2009, p.115)

Allowing children the opportunity to learn more about the world they live in enables them to have a better chance at success and be understanding and respectful of others. This therefore means that educators need to give all children, especially those who are disadvantaged, opportunities that they may not be exposed to outside their early years setting. When a child walks through your doors, the opportunities you give them could be far greater than any they may have access to otherwise, so all that you do is vital in narrowing the gap and ensuring that all children can succeed and be confident individuals.

I want to share a story about a young child called Callum, who came from a disadvantaged family with low income. Callum was one of six children all under the age of eight years and was in the bottom set in his class for reading, writing and mathematics. I met Callum when I was doing some part-time work in his year 2 class at a school in England. He was quiet and I noticed him straightaway. Callum was already at a disadvantage and his teacher was too busy with the rest of the class to give enough attention to those who needed it the most, like Callum. I decided to support all the children sitting on the table who were classed as the 'bottom of the class' – not great for their confidence to begin with. The children were given a writing task of short sentences, and Callum's writing was far below where it should have been; his words all ran into each other, his letter sizes were taking up two if not three lines, and they sloped diagonally down the page. I knew that he was capable of so much more if someone could just give him the time and support, so I asked his class teacher if I could do some one-to-one work with him, which she was reluctant for me to do because he didn't 'qualify for additional support', but I persisted.

I spent 20 minutes with Callum, showing him how to form letters correctly using funny rhymes and using his finger as a 'space invader' to separate his words. I showed Callum how to fit his letters on the line, and the progress he made from just 20 minutes of dedicated support was unbelievable. I supported Callum through this piece of work, and we compared how this looked with his previous work – he had a beaming smile on his face because this little boy felt as if he could achieve. Callum then proceeded to show his work to every teacher he could find because he was so proud of himself. This 20-minute session gave Callum the opportunity to realize his potential and helped to set the bar at what he was actually capable of. In the weeks following this, it was clear that this little boy needed nurturing, supporting and guiding – he needed someone to believe in him rather than think he was a lost cause.

My time with Callum was short but I know that it made a difference because of his amazing progress in just a few short weeks. We need to build confidence, self-esteem and courage, as children like Callum need the support of their teachers. Early education flies past us and those first five years of life impact on a child's future success and achievements. The experiences we can provide will have a lasting effect, so give children your time and patience and never give up on any of them.

I truly believe that if you have one adult in your life who is your cheerleader and who believes in you then it is far easier to have a growth mindset, be resilient and have that grit, determination and courage because somebody believes in you. If you don't have anyone that truly supports you and builds your confidence, it is far easier to give up and not move forward. I'll be honest, there were times when I thought I couldn't write this book but writing this chapter on not giving up certainly did help!

Challenges and hardships are really tough – they test us but we learn so much from them. Carol Dweck (2016, p.33) stated, 'Even in the growth mindset, failure can be a painful experience. But it doesn't define you. It's a problem to be faced, dealt with, and learned from.' When teaching our young children, we have to let them know that challenges are difficult and they can be a really hard and painful experience to go through, which is why children especially need that support from an adult. Once you have had that support as a child, when you face those challenges as an adult you are far more equipped to deal with them, because you know that you will overcome and benefit from the experience in some way.

Cultural capital means giving children opportunities and experiences to be knowledgeable about the world around them. When you feel as though you understand something, you are more confident in yourself. We must show our children that they can accomplish their dreams and that opportunities are available for everyone, regardless of their background. Going back to Callum, the little boy I mentioned earlier, I asked him what he wanted to be when he was older and he told me that he wanted to be a dinner lady like the ladies in the kitchen at his school. They were some of the biggest role models in Callum's life and I don't think he had anyone to talk to him about the endless possibilities the world has to offer or the alternative aspirations he could have. I raised the bar for Callum and posed the question, 'Well, that is a great idea. If you want to be a chef, what about if you had your very own restaurant?' Callum looked at me bewildered and said, 'Could I do that?' I told Callum that of course he could and we had a rich conversation about the food he likes and the type of restaurant he would have… suddenly this little boy's world became a little bigger and the opportunities became a little greater.

Never underestimate the impact you can have on a child.

Reflection

Let's re-cap on this chapter and reflect on the themes spoken about. Write your answers down in your scrapbook so you can look back on them in the future and create a working reflection book. It will really help you when you face challenges in the future and can remind yourself how you felt before and how you felt when you overcame your challenges. This is a really great tool to support your own growth and development!

Self-reflection

1. When have you faced a challenge in your personal life or career?

2. How did this challenge make you feel during and after?

3. What did you learn from this challenge? Did you overcome it?

4. Have you faced a challenge that you decided to give up on? How did you feel about this?

5. As a child, did you have somebody who encouraged and supported you through challenges? How did this impact on you?

6. As an adult, do you have somebody who supports you? How do they help you?

7. How are you resilient?

Teaching reflection

1. How do you support your children to keep on trying?

2. How do you encourage your children to be resilient?

3. When has a child you taught given up? What did you do?

4. How do you provide your children with challenges? Is there more that you could do?

5. Think of a time a child needed support. Did you step in too quickly or did you give them time to try to figure it out?

6. Do your children think critically? Do they make links and show a willingness to 'have a go'?

7. Do you raise awareness of the importance of a growth mindset to your colleagues and children's parents? How could you do this?

CHAPTER 3

Forest School and Outdoor Education

The outdoor environment offers children endless opportunities for growing and learning in all areas of development. Before I became a Forest School leader I remember first hearing about this way of teaching and I was curious to find out more. I never like to be stuck in the same place for long and get fed up of being indoors, especially in a room that is busy and noisy. When I looked back on my fondest memories of my childhood I noticed a particular pattern, so I decided to ask a group of adults varying in age from 22 to 82 about their fondest memories. Can you guess what everyone's answers were (and yes, they were all the same!)? 'Being outside', 'Playing outside with my friends', 'Building dens in our garden', 'Exploring and going on adventures'. Immediately, everyone referred to experiences they had had outside, and recalled these tales with such happiness.

I trained as a Forest School leader in 2015 with Patrick Harrison who runs Greenbow Training. I can honestly say that it was the most incredible training I have ever done, and a week in the forest learning how to appreciate and connect with the natural world felt like a week of therapy. No technology, no emails to respond to or calls to answer, I was completely in the moment and savouring every aspect. If you are thinking of training to become a Forest School leader, do it, you will not regret it. It changed my mindset and outlook on education and life, it made me realize what is really important and how refreshed and calm being outside makes you feel.

Children need to spend quality time outside daily as it reduces stressors, allows them to explore, discover and play more freely, as well as using up any built-up energy! In nurseries and preschool environments, indoor classrooms can become noisy, stuffy and over-stimulating after a period of time, which can heighten children's stress levels and affect their ability to regulate their emotions. When more than one sense is in overdrive, it can trigger children to have what we call a 'meltdown' because they can't cope with the overload of processing so much information. When children get to this point, they cannot learn and play effectively, which is why, whatever the weather, children need time outside daily, and 'there is no such thing as bad weather, just bad clothing'. Embracing the rain, going mud sliding, splashing in puddles and feeling the raindrops on their face – it will energize them!

I know that most people's instant reaction when they hear the term 'Forest School' is to picture a school or cabin situated in the middle of a woodland and I am sorry to break it to you but that is not entirely true. First and foremost, 'Forest School' is an ethos. It provides us as adults and children with the opportunity to connect or re-connect with the world around us in its natural state. It gives us the space and freedom away from time pressures, technology and the stress of everyday life to reflect on ourselves in our basic form.

Being outdoors enables exploration, discovery and understanding, not just of the physical, natural world and its resources that are visible but of ourselves on an emotional and psychological level. It allows us to find our inner confidence. Forest School is a continuous long-term programme that allows us to be reflective, make mistakes and connections and have balance within our everyday lives. Ideally, Forest School sessions would take place in a wooded area but they can equally be done in any outdoor space if you are a little creative.

Another belief people have is that Forest School is all about lighting fires and using tools, when in fact these are just elements of it. Settings that use the same site for Forest School will typically have a designated fire area and will teach their children about fire safety, fire lighting and cooking methods. There really is nothing better than sitting around a fire, reading stories, cooking and eating lunch and reflecting on your day. However, some Forest School sessions may hardly ever light fires or use them, as it is just one 'element'. Similarly, bushcraft is another element of Forest School, where children are taught how to use tools safely to make and create furniture and woodland toys and to learn new skills and crafts.

Holistic teaching

One way in which I would describe Forest School and outdoor learning is 'holistic', a term we looked at in Chapter 1. It focuses on all the needs of the child rather than just one or two areas.

The environment itself offers great opportunities for learning, exploration, discovery and risk-taking. The educator can then develop session plans that build on what the natural environment already supplies, ensuring that they are flexible and offer spontaneity and natural personal discovery for each participant. It is important that each educator is aware of when their support and guidance are necessary for each child; for example, demonstrating safe use of equipment or supporting an activity. However, this help could be needed at different times for different children. Sometimes too much help does not support the process of developing a growth mindset and determination to face challenges, but instead teaches that you know better or don't have confidence that the child is able to accomplish that task themselves.

I want to introduce you to another framework called SPICES (not the kind you find in your cooking!), which again has that holistic approach and supports all development areas. It stands for Social, Physical, Intellectual, Communication, Emotional and Spiritual. It is useful to know and apply when thinking about planning activities and ideas.

SPICES is broken down like this:

- Social: Forest School enables children to interact with each other through play. It offers the opportunity to support each other during activities, work as a team and interact with different children.

- Physical: Forest School gives opportunities to support fine and gross motor skills and development. Gross motor skills include skills such as climbing, running and managing the space around themselves. Fine motor skills include skills such as whittling, threading and tying knots.

- Intellectual: Forest School allows opportunities to broaden knowledge about the world around us, life cycles, seasons, flora and fauna. It encourages problem solving through a range of activities, using trial and error, exploration and discovery. It also allows children to share experiences and learn from others.

- Communication: Forest School allows children the chance to communicate verbally and non-verbally with their peers and teachers. Communication leads to knowledge development, social interaction, creative ideas, imaginative skills, play, reflection and consolidation.

- Emotional: Forest School provides the foundations to build on personal emotional intelligence and wellbeing; it allows children to realize talents and strengths they didn't know they had but also to see where their difficulties lie and how to overcome them. Forest School also allows children to support each other, evolving empathy skills and emotional connections with their peers, themselves and the world around them.

- Spiritual: Forest School enables children to make connections with the world around them and also within themselves on a psychological level. It enables them to express themselves, their ideas and their views.

Enabling environment

Forest School fosters resilient, confident, independent and creative learners because of its supportive, equal and holistic nature.

When children explore, they discover new things and when they can do that by themselves their sense of achievement is so great you can see first-hand their self-esteem and confidence rising by the minute! It allows them to believe that they can create their own learning, follow their interests and become independent – always knowing that you, the teacher, are there if they need you. Learning happens best when it is fun and also incidental.

Lily had just joined a Forest School nursery, a very different setting from what she was used to. Lily's parents felt as though her previous nursery was not the right environment for her; she was confident and sociable at home and quiet and shy when there, so they made the decision to move her. In the beginning, as you would expect, Lily would stick near an adult and observe the other children and how they explored the woodlands, climbing, running, jumping, foraging and playing. The weeks passed and Lily became more confident, gentle reassurance and encouragement from her teachers supporting her to feel more relaxed and able to begin exploring and interacting with the other children. The child Lily's parents had described at home was beginning to appear at Forest School too. The environment allowed Lily to feel safe, calm and secure and enabled her learning and allowed her to be herself.

From this story, it is important to recognize that because an environment or setting works for some children, it does not mean it will work for everyone. As educators, it is important that we look out for these signs so that we can support children in reaching their potential. An enabling environment can look different for each child – some children like noisy, busy environments and others prefer quiet and calming environments. I know for a fact that being in crowded places with lots of noise pushes my senses into overdrive after a while and I cannot wait to get away! I love London but after a busy day in the city I enjoy nothing more than having a quiet walk through the countryside, yet I have friends who could never live anywhere but the city, and who thrive on the buzz and energy. What works for one person, does not always work for another...

Natural resources

Nature provides us with so much and is the basis of our existence, yet so often we spend far too much money on buying resources and activities for our children when we can create rich activities and opportunities for learning through the world around us. One of my favourite activities is natural art, as the possibilities are endless and children can be free in their creations. What can you make out of a pile of leaves, stones and grass?

Not only are children able to explore their surroundings to gather natural resources and learn about different trees, wildflowers and embellishments, they can also explore piecing them together to create their own kind of art. This type of activity is just as much about the process as the final product, which should always be their own interpretation – there is no right or wrong way to be creative.

A lion?   *A portrait?*

A mandala?   *A dog?*

Outdoor activity ideas

Working in early education means you will be no stranger to the importance of the outdoor environment, but when society has been so focused on education being taught in an indoor environment, teachers can be afraid of the unknown and how to become creative outdoors. Which is why I want to share some great activity ideas with you, to help you feel more confident teaching outside. Remember, not all classrooms have four walls…

Fairy tales bring adventure, magic and imagination to young children – a great recipe for learning through play! Children become fascinated with make-believe as their innocence allows them to believe in every possibility, while creating and engaging in play with their peers and teachers. Children need to be engaged and excited in order to learn, and sparking that imagination is a great way to do it.

I often create small letters from fairies, pixies or made up mythical characters and hide them in the woodlands, parks or nursery gardens for the children I am teaching to find. The joy and anticipation on finding one of these letters is just wonderful and the children become engaged, animated and excited to find out what the letter says…

Dear Children, my name is Lily the Woodland Fairy. My friend Sneeze, who is a very friendly Dragon has had a terrible cold which has made him sneeze even more than normal! Yesterday he accidently sneezed and blew away our Fairy village! Do you think you could work together and help to rebuild it? Love Lily the Woodland Fairy

This simple letter can be the start of a fantastic activity, full of exploration and learning. Teachers can get involved and build part of the fairy village too, as it will support the children with their ideas and knowledge about how to use the natural resources. Using sticks to create structures, moss and leaves to make carpets, stones for borders…the possibilities are endless.

ACTIVITY: Build a fairy home

What you will need:

- two 'y' shaped sticks that are similar in height

- one long stick

- eight+ sticks

- leaves or bracken

- moss

- stones, feathers, flowers and any other resources you can find

- small world characters (it doesn't have to be just for fairies).

Make your fairy home:

1. Show the children what a 'y' shaped stick looks like and ask them to find two 'y' shaped sticks in your outdoor space.

2. Place the ends of the 'y' sticks into the ground, close to each other – the further apart they are the bigger the house is going to be.

3. Show the children a longer stick that will be used to balance across both 'y' sticks, joining them together to make the frame of the house.

4. Next invite the children to gather eight sticks of a similar height. These sticks will be used to make the

wall of the fairy home. Balance each stick diagonally against the long stick, keeping them close together.

5. Encourage the children to think about resources they could find to help keep the home waterproof, like moss. Use these to place over the top of the home.

6. Once they have finished decorating, the fairy home is ready to play with. Take some small-world toys to support their role-playing and invite the children to tell each other about their home and how they made it. It will surprise you how different they all will be!

7. Most importantly, allow the children to make their own creations as it builds their self-confidence and personal skills. I am never too worried about a session going exactly as I had planned because children are fluid and I want them to lead their own paths. Usually, the fairy villages end up far better than I could have ever imagined! No mind works the same, so it is crucial to be flexible and give the children the opportunity to express their ideas and design; for example, I would have never thought about the necessity for a village washing line!

Another example of how to include fairy tales in the natural environment is to use the power of children's books. I will read *The Gruffalo* (Donaldson and Scheffler 1999) for example, in the woods to the children first and then begin to extend the story by asking the children if they would like to help build the homes for all the characters in the book (snake, fox and owl) using natural resources. Once the children are engaged in the activity (and it is ok if some don't want to participate, as spontaneous play is hugely beneficial) then it is a great opportunity to 'act out' the whole story from start to finish as a group, moving around, using different voices and having fun!

Outdoor activities and the Early Years Foundation Stage

I would argue that any outdoor activity can relate to most, if not all, areas of the EYFS. A simple yet effective activity like the one based on *The Gruffalo* supports all of the EYFS areas, including the specific, and here's how:

- *Personal, social and emotional:* The children are interacting socially and are learning how to share and turn-take with the resources and their ideas. They have to use their empathy skills to support each other and build on their emotional intelligences.

- *Communication and language:* The children are communicating with each other and the teacher to broadcast their ideas, using verbal and non-verbal means. The storytelling allows for rich language to be heard and understood.

- *Physical:* The outdoor environment provides a wealth of physical activity; the children are moving and handling resources, walking, running and navigating the space around them.

- *Mathematics:* The children are building, making shapes and counting how many logs snake needs for his home.

- *Understanding of the world:* The children are in the natural world to begin with, so they are taking in their surroundings, finding insects as they move logs, noticing the changes of the seasons and the plants growing or decaying.

- *Literacy:* The children read the story from start to finish, immersing themselves in it by acting it out and living the story through movement and voice.

- *Expressive arts and design:* This activity ignites children's imagination and they will incidentally evolve the story and continue in play after the main activity has ended.

Forest School should be a 'safe' place for all children to get away from everyday life stressors and ordeals and have a time where they can forget, feel equal and progress.

Forest School and risk-taking

Spending time outdoors in a natural environment over time has a positive effect on mental health and wellbeing. It allows children to become resilient and know that making mistakes is a good thing in order to learn and progress. It also encourages children to feel relaxed and calm because those everyday life stressors are removed. I have never had a child ask to use any kind of technology when out in the woods as they are always so content with what is around them.

Tying in the with the growth mindset approach again, Forest School really supports that confidence building and resilience because there are always opportunities for taking managed risks. Climbing, balancing, using tools, carrying resources, building, fire lighting, exploring…the list is endless. Each time a child takes a risk it not only builds on their physical strengths and abilities but also their confidence and self-esteem as they have to carefully plan and manage themselves when they take risks, which has a huge benefit to their overall development. As Roald Dahl so perfectly put it, 'The more risks you allow children to take, the better they learn to take care of themselves' (1993). And, indeed, it is true. When we are giving that opportunity to risk-take, it allows us to learn so much, including how to care for ourselves and have a better awareness of what is going on, rather than always relying on somebody else because we have not had the opportunity to experience it.

When we look at risk we have to be logical and sensible. This diagram of the 'zones of risk' explains this perfectly.

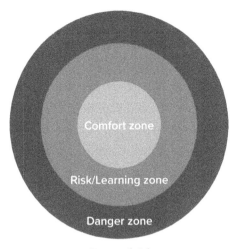

Zones of risk

When you put yourself out of your comfort zone, extraordinary things can happen, but we have to be mindful and risk-assess before we do so to ensure that we are not putting ourselves or our children in the 'danger' zone. We have to test our limits and our capabilities – which are all individual to each person – and take a sensible approach to this. When was the last time you took a risk or stepped out of your comfort zone and something wonderful happened? Afterwards, I bet you thought 'Why was I so worried about doing that!'

Overall, it is not just about 'Forest School' but outdoor education of any kind. They both foster resilient, confident, independent and creative learners because of their supportive, equal and holistic nature.

Forest School is about a personal journey of discovery and progression. The woodlands provide a natural environment full of resources in their most basic form. This in the first instance is a challenge, as some children will not be used to being outside in all weathers and in an environment less familiar, so this will test their strengths and allow them to become more resilient to the cold and wet (for example) as time goes on because they will learn how to adapt.

Forest School offers a fantastic environment to build confidence. A child who is unfamiliar with being in a natural environment may be unsure of their physical abilities, and climbing a tree could be something that is very daunting to them. With encouragement and development of spatial awareness skills, that child will be supported to climb a little further each session, building their confidence steadily. Once a child understands that they can accomplish and achieve when supported, it gives them a 'wow' moment of realization, and the determination to apply that theory to another situation. This therefore builds their inner confidence and self-esteem.

Creativity is vital, and children should have every opportunity to be creative and know that their creations are unique and important. At Forest School, children have an area to explore and discover and they will often begin creating their own imaginative play; with prompts and involvement with their peers, these games will extend and progress, allowing a flow of creativity. One example is a tree being turned into a spaceship, where a child invites their peers to fly to the moon to find aliens, using sticks as a steering wheel for their spacecraft and spotting 'bush' aliens. This type of play encourages not only creativity but also social skills, confidence, physical ability, communication and emotional intelligence. Creativity can also be developing a natural art picture on the ground, starting with a stick and evolving it to create a large piece of art, individual to each child or group of children.

Children become independent because the teacher is there to facilitate the sessions, provide some ideas, opportunities and resources, but the children are encouraged to discover and make decisions and choices themselves without constant approval from the leader. This wholly supports independence and constructive thinking for each individual as well as building confidence and resilience.

There is a reason that so many of our fondest childhood memories are of being outside, exploring, discovering and playing – it is where we had the most fun!

Reflection

First, take some time to reflect on this chapter – go for a walk outside and immerse yourself in nature. How did you feel before and how do you feel afterwards? When was the last time you reconnected with yourself and focused on your wellbeing? Being outside really helps up to ground ourselves and refocus, even just for 20 minutes!

Self-reflection

1. Look back and write down your fondest childhood memories. Is there a pattern? How does it make you feel remembering those moments?

2. How often to do you spend time outdoors? How does it make you feel when you do?

3. If you don't spend time outside often, I urge you to try going for a walk once a day and writing down how you felt before and afterwards.

4. When was the last time you took a risk or stepped out of your comfort zone? What happened? How did you feel before and afterwards?

Teaching reflection

1. Can you reflect on an activity or lesson that focused on the whole child? How did this work?

2. If you have not used a holistic approach, make some notes on how you might like to try this in the future. Note down some ideas and try them out! Don't worry if it doesn't go to plan – remember, mistakes = learning!

3. Look at the children in your teaching group. How does your environment support them? What are their strengths and weaknesses?

4. How can you create an enabling environment to support all of your children?

5. How do your children behave during indoor and outdoor sessions? Is there any difference?

6. Sometimes it is not the activity that is wrong, but the environment. Can you think of a time when this could be true for you?

7. Have you used natural resources to support play and learning? If not, try out some natural art or building woodland homes! Reflect on how the children reacted during and after these sessions.

8. Allow your children to take carefully managed risks over a period of time and note down the progress and changes in their behaviour, confidence and resilience when doing this.

CHAPTER 4

Emotional Intelligence

Emotions control our lives daily, we react to people, situations, places, food… Who would dispute the sheer pleasure in taking a bite into our favourite food? We are overcome with emotions of happiness and pleasure. And then there is the sheer pain when we have to say goodbye to a loved one and the tidal wave of sadness that sweeps our bodies. Our entire existence is based on our emotions, so when we can understand them better we can cope when life throws us situations where our emotions run away with us.

A simplified version of the dictionary's definition of 'emotional intelligence' is: the ability to express and control your emotions, while also having an awareness of other people's emotions and how to handle them with thought and empathy. To be 'emotionally intelligent' we have first to understand the different types of emotions and how they can affect us, as well as know how to talk about them and what to do when we experience those emotions. Not only that, we have to pick up on other people's state of emotions and understand those social cues too.

Remember the multiple intelligence theory all the way back in Chapter 1? Well two of those eight intelligences relate and fit together with this idea of emotional intelligence. Yes, you guessed it, 'intra-personal' and 'inter-personal'. Let me give you a quick recap:

- intra-personal: connecting with your inner feeling and emotions

- inter-personal: relationships, communicating with others and understanding emotional cues.

Now this is where it gets super exciting (I hope you are beginning to see how all of these chapters interlock with each other!). Let me break it down even further.

Daniel Goleman, an American psychologist, categorized emotional intelligence into five areas (Cherry 2019) which fit perfectly within the intra- and inter-personal skills:

Intra-personal skills:

- *Self-awareness:* This is the ability to take note of ourselves (reflection), to not let our feelings take over and to understand our strengths and weaknesses.

- *Self-regulation:* This is the ability to stay calm, focused and alert to our emotions, ensuring that we control impulses and think about how we feel before reacting.

- *Self-motivation:* This is the ability to be motivated to satisfy expectation or a goal without being influenced by another to do so. You are happy to wait for long-term success rather than strive for immediate results.

Inter-personal skills:

- *Empathy:* This is the ability to be aware of other people's feelings and emotions and how to respond to them in a supportive and caring manner – to put yourself in their shoes.

- *Social skills:* This is the ability to communicate with someone, converse, turn-take and be involved (eye contact).

Until recently, we have been more inclined not to talk about our emotions and how we are feeling as adults, as it was always seen as a sign of weakness rather than a strength. Thankfully, emotional wellbeing and good mental health have been a huge focus in recent years, a change that has most definitely been needed. When we can recognize and understand our emotions, we are able to regulate them and react to situations with more awareness, also enabling us to interpret and respond to others more effectively.

So, before we can teach children about emotions we need to educate ourselves to be more in touch with how we are feeling and why – this is self-reflection. For example, if I leave planning or organizing an activity to the last minute, it may stress me out and cause me to feel uptight and anxious. If I then start a session with a group of children feeling anxious and uptight, they will pick up on this energy and it most likely will not go to plan.

Teaching children about emotions

Those who work with and care for young children will be very familiar with a toddler 'meltdown', a situation where the child is so overcome with emotion that they cannot regulate their feelings and the impact is too great so they break down, usually crying, screaming and throwing themselves to the ground. 'And the Oscar for most dramatic performance goes to…'. But in all seriousness they reach a point where no matter how trivial the situation they simply cannot deal with the raw emotion that hits them so suddenly. A child can be content and happy and then when you, for example, stop them from painting their friend's hair and the kitchen walls, they are struck by this overwhelming emotion, and go from zero to 100 in the blink of an eye. It is because they have not developed the skills to rationalize the situation and regulate their responses – this is all new and they are still testing out the boundaries.

This really is a normal reaction because it takes time for children to understand and work out how to regulate themselves and this is only achieved with the support of an adult. When children reach this point, I always find it useful to tune into my emotions and see how their reaction/behaviour/crying makes me feel. Typically, the emotion you feel in response to the child is a projection of how they are feeling. You know the difference between a distressed cry that sends shivers down your spine and one that encompasses complete frustration. This has certainly helped to guide my reactions to dealing with situations and supporting the child to regulate themselves.

Children need adults to guide and teach them about their emotions. The more we understand, the more we can do. I therefore suggest that talking about emotions becomes part of your everyday teaching; it needs to be embedded into your curriculum. Discuss with the children how you feel and invite them to talk about their emotions too. I am sure a lot of adults would agree that if they had been given the opportunity to speak about their emotions freely as a child they would not struggle so much now as an adult or have emotions stored up that they never faced or dealt with, simply because it was 'not the done thing'.

Here is a list of good phrases to encourage children to talk about their emotions and to connect a feeling to an emotion:

'I can see that you are upset; can you tell me what has made you feel upset?'

'It is ok to feel angry, but it is not ok to...'

'Can I help you to feel calm again?'

'How you feel right now will not last forever – we all feel different emotions.'

'I am going to be right here waiting and if you need me let me know.'

'Feeling worried is normal, and everybody feels like this sometimes.'

'What happened before you felt like this?'

'How does this make you feel?'

'Let's sit down and take some time to feel calm.'

'It is ok to feel jealous, this is a feeling we all get sometimes.'

It is important to let children know that all emotions and feelings are normal and that everyone experiences them from time to time.

Now let's look at the intra-personal side of emotional intelligence, and how to support children to be self-aware and to self-regulate. As the teacher, I have picture references or toys that represent all of the emotions, so children have a visual aid while we discuss an emotion. These emotions include:

- happy

- excited

- sad

- worried

- bored

- angry

- grumpy

- jealous

- scared

- quiet

- embarrassed

- shy.

When you have your list of emotions and visual cues that represent them you can choose to do an activity – three examples are given below.

ACTIVITY 1: Role play

Using small-world toys, act out scenarios with the child (children) to demonstrate different emotions and feelings. The scenarios could be written on cards that the children can select: 'The farmer has lost his cow. How does he feel?' The adult demonstrates this using the small-world toys and the child has to respond. As the child becomes more confident, take turns to demonstrate the actions.

ACTIVITY 2: Books

I highly recommend the Molly Potter (2014, 2018) books, *What's Worrying You?* and *How Are You Feeling Today?* as they not only discuss different emotions but also give strategies on what to do when you feel each of those emotions, which are really helpful tools to support children in self-regulation. They also give scenarios of when you might feel a certain way – for example, when you get a new teacher you may feel sad, anxious, upset or nervous – alongside positive things to remember about this situation.

I also frequently use children's picture books in different ways to support emotional intelligence. I may not read the story at all but just look at the illustrations and ask the child to talk about how the characters might be feeling, so they can be in tune with physical responses to emotions. Or I read the story and then go back through the book asking the child how the characters were feeling at different points and why. This helps to get them thinking while being engaged in a story that they enjoy!

ACTIVITY 3: Improvisation

Sometime simple is the best! Take all of those visual emotion cards and in a group encourage the children to act out each emotion. As the teacher, I always over-exaggerate the emotion to really get the point across! To make it more fun you can add a set of cards with animal names on them, so you take one animal card and one emotion card: 'We all have to walk around like angry lions!' You get the idea!

Supporting emotional wellbeing

Children need to form strong attachments and emotional bonds with key people in their lives, such as their parents, close relatives and teachers, in order to feel safe and secure. Children's brains develop rapidly, especially through their first year of life, and those children who have formed strong attachments develop wiring or connectors in the brain that support their future ability to make positive relationships with others. Young children need love, reassurance and emotional support from their caregivers in order to learn and develop well.

This is why the Early Years Foundation Stage puts great importance on the role of a 'key person' for all children who attend early years settings. It is a statutory requirement that they have someone with whom they can build a relationship, who can meet their individual needs and ensure that they feel safe and secure – otherwise learning will not take place effectively.

Children need to know that we are there and we care about their wellbeing; educators need to offer emotional support to young children so that they feel reassured and can ask for help if they need to. Educators need to demonstrate that they are 'present' in the moment and ask questions or make statements to show they are engaged with the child: 'How are you today?', 'If you need any help, I am just here,' 'What would you like to do today?', 'What is your favourite thing to play with?' These are simple questions that build foundations for a relationship and trust.

Listen. Show a child that you are interested in what they have to say, and allow them the time to explain or express themselves so you can demonstrate empathy and good communication skills that they will then pick up on and model in the future. Listening and attention skills are a huge part of social communication and understanding how others are thinking and feeling, which goes a long way in supporting that emotional intelligence and awareness.

Allowing children the opportunity to make those vital mistakes in their development and learning enhances their emotional wellbeing in the future as they can recover from failure and know that it is a positive step towards achieving their goals. Each time we fail, we are a step closer to success.

Allow children the opportunity to be in an environment that enhances their emotional wellbeing rather than over-stimulates it. Children need to have balance within their day and have places to go where they can relax and feel calm, which affects their emotional state and overall happiness. Children should always have a quiet, safe place they can retire to when they need peace and to restore their emotional balance.

Teaching children about kindness and empathy

Kindness is one of the founding qualities that everyone should possess. Kindness needs a great deal of emotional thought and awareness and requires selflessness and genuine care and love towards others. Kindness offers emotional support to others and shows them that you care and are invested in that person's emotional wellbeing too.

I teach children about kindness from as early an age as possible, demonstrating how to share and use gentle hands when there are really young infants and then building up to doing selfless tasks and expressing nice comments about someone or something. One of the best ways to teach kindness is to model it yourself as the educator.

One of my favourite books to use with children from the age of three or four years is *Have You Filled a Bucket Today?* by Carol McCloud (2006). It is truly a fantastic book that teaches young children how to show kindness towards others and that when we do this it not only makes the other person feel happy, it makes us feel happy too. The book is centred around the idea that every person has an invisible bucket that they carry around with them every day, and when the bucket is full we feel happy and when the bucket is empty we feel sad. People can be bucket fillers or bucket dippers; when we show kindness we help to fill other people's buckets and our own, but when we are mean or say something hurtful we become a bucket dipper and dip into someone else's bucket and our own. I really love this book because it gives great visuals for children to clearly understand how to be kind and the effects that kindness has on us and others. The book is a great starting point to help support you in creating a wealth of activity ideas and opportunities centered around kindness.

When somebody walks into a room and smiles at you, it makes you feel good – smiles are contagious! Compliments are a perfect way to make someone feel happy and show that you are thinking of them: 'I really like your shoes today' or 'I thought you did a fantastic job planting in the garden today.' Teaching children small gestures of kindness will not only make them feel good but show them the correct behaviour to display towards others.

All of these kindness acts enable children to be in touch with their emotions and the emotions of others, promoting social communication and relationship building which are vital skills for future success and development.

Philosophy for children

This is another great tool to support children's emotional intelligence and wellbeing. The idea is to enhance children's abilities to think, have opinions, listen to others and reason.

One of the ways in which I do this is to read a story that has a theme, like friendship for example, and then in a circle invite the children to answer questions that I give them. The role of the teacher is to not agree or disagree – they must stay completely impartial so that the children develop their own ideas without fear of being right or wrong (confidence building), and the teacher thanks them for sharing their thoughts. It takes a lot of courage and confidence to say what you think and feel in front of your peers but if we can encourage children to do this from a young age then it will be far easier and 'normal' for them as they grow up. It also encourages them to listen to their peers and wait their turn to speak, and to realize that everyone's opinion is valued and should be heard.

Typically I ask open-ended questions like:

'How did the book make you feel?'

'How do you think the rabbit felt?'

'What would you do?'

'Was it right or wrong for the elephant to…'

It is very interesting to hear their views and opinions. Some children may not want to offer anything initially but once they realize that it is a safe space they always end up joining in eventually. The key is to not put any pressure on them.

Another way in which you can use the philosophy circle is to show children confusing pictures and let them begin a discussion around them (not giving any ideas or preferences as the adult, but just enabling the activity), for example a picture of a chocolate teapot or a bike with square wheels! The ideas and thoughts that photos like these bring are fantastic! 'Will it be hard or easy to ride a bike with square wheels?' Powerful images can spark children's critical thinking and engagement, and allowing them the freedom to express their thoughts without fear of getting it wrong is fundamental. Can you remember a time when you were in a group situation, perhaps at a training event or back in college or school, and the teacher asked a question to the class – you were 95 per cent sure you knew the answer but the self-doubt crept in and you feared getting it wrong and didn't want to feel silly in front of everyone? So you kept quiet and the confident person who had answered most of the questions gave the answer and you were right all along! We have all been there and kicked ourselves for not saying what we thought! It is that fear of getting it wrong that can stop us in our tracks. This is why, if we teach children from a young age that it is ok to express our thoughts and opinions in a group situation without that fear or judgement, it will build their confidence and help them to realize that nothing bad is going to happen when they do share.

Philosophy really enables young children to engage with their emotions, their awareness of their thoughts, feelings and views, as well as those of their peers. It is a wonderful tool for encouraging positive relationships, discussion and debate.

Once we are aware of our own emotions we can become aware of and understand others' emotions. Communication, empathy and kindness help to build attachments between peers and allow children to offer emotional support to each other through friendship – a vital skill for future development and learning.

ACTIVITY: Emotions reflection box

Activity aims: To support children's understanding of emotions by connecting their real experiences to the different types of emotion we all encounter. This activity encourages children to voice their ideas and thoughts among their peers without fear of being judged. It supports their listening and attention skills and social communication and confidence. Lastly, it supports critical thinking, questioning and debating skills, as children make connections and challenge their thoughts.

- As a group, create and decorate a 'reflections box' where the children can post their reflective drawings or messages. It is somewhere they can store their thoughts and feelings.

- Invite the children to sit together in a circle (outside or inside) and remind them that while in our philosophy circle we share our ideas and take turns to speak by putting our hand up or out in front of us (this is a nice way to show you want to offer your thoughts). You could also use a physical object that indicates when someone is speaking – this can be especially helpful when a group is new to an activity like this.

- Choose an emotion to discuss as your theme for this session and a picture book that you can use to accompany this emotion. For example, if the emotion was 'fear', *The Gruffalo* (Donaldson and Scheffler 1999) would be a good book to use. You can begin by introducing the emotion to the children, perhaps with a picture cue to go with it, and invite the children to talk about what they think 'fear' is.

- Read your chosen story to the group. Once you have read the story, ask the children some questions relating to the emotion, connecting it with the story to start with:

  - 'How do you think the animals felt when they saw the gruffalo?'

  - 'How would you feel if you saw the gruffalo?'

  - 'What would you do?'

- Extend the questions to relate the emotion to a personal experience, recalling an event. You could offer an example yourself to begin with, 'I once felt scared when I... Can you think of a time when you were scared or fearful?' It is important also to explore with the children ideas for how to respond to this particular emotion when they feel it and to explain that all emotions are 'normal' and we experience them all at some point.

- Invite the children once they have shared and discussed their thoughts and emotions to draw or paint a picture of the emotion. They can then share these with each other or simply post them straight into the reflection box. The physical act of doing this helps children to recall an event, connect with the emotion and understand how to respond to the emotion when they feel it again.

- Always thank the children for their contributions – never show a preferred style or answer but thank everyone. Even if a child's contribution is not about the topic, praise them for their confidence in speaking out. It is likely that they may have summoned the confidence to speak out but about a topic they are comfortable with at that time, and with encouragement that confidence will build and they will feel able to explore the discussions at hand.

- You can repeat this activity with different emotions, perhaps even creating an emotions collage of the children's art work if they are happy to display it.

Reflection

Understanding our emotions can be tricky, especially if we are not used to doing it. Take some time to think about how you connect or could connect more with your emotions so that you can then engage and support your children further.

Self-reflection

1. How do you connect with your inner feelings and emotions? Think of a time you did this and what impact it had.

2. How do you respond to others and pick up on their emotional cues? Are you aware? Or could you be more aware?

3. How do you regulate your own emotions when faced with a situation?

4. Have you ever acted on impulse as a result of an emotion? How did that work out – positively or negatively?

5. Can you reflect on a situation where your emotions changed and caused an effect on others? What did you do?

Teaching reflection

1. Think about a time when a child has been upset/angry/frustrated. How did their emotions make you feel and how did you respond?

2. How do you support children to understand their emotions?

3. Reflect on a time when a child has had a 'meltdown' – why do you think this was? What was the situation and how did you support them to regulate their emotions? How could you have supported them better?

4. Do you listen enough and make yourself present for your children? Do they have the opportunity to talk about how they feel? What could you do to support them further?

CHAPTER 5

The Reflective Practitioner

What does it mean to be reflective? It is all about looking back on yourself and taking the time to review your actions, emotions, behaviour, teaching – it can be in any aspect of your life. When we have the ability to self-reflect we can improve and learn from previous situations – there is always room for improvement. I try to remind myself that life continuously moves forwards and in order for us to do the same and progress we have to work and change too. Self-reflection can be daunting to begin with but fearing change will prevent continued success and growth. As psychologist Abraham Maslow stated, 'You will either step forward into growth or you will step back into safety' (Dempsey 2010, p.14).

Reflection is so important within our lives and is an element that connects with each of the themes within this book. Reflecting on ourselves as well as our children ensures we support them as best as we can. Building children's confidence, resilience and emotional intelligence requires self-reflection too; we have to look back and learn from past experiences, connecting with how we felt at the time in order to move forwards and progress. Throughout the book, we have been self-reflecting at the end of the chapters. I wanted to do this so that you can connect your own personal experiences to the topics that are discussed. In this way, the book becomes more meaningful to you and your life, and especially how you take all of this information forwards to benefit you and your children.

If you take a look at any successful business or person, they have developed their ideas and work in order to keep progressing. Take the Virgin Group, owned by Richard Branson, a global brand that is worth over five billion pounds. When the business started doing well, Branson certainly did not just say, 'Well, that's it, we have mastered it, no need to do any more!' because if he had done, Virgin would not have progressed, developed and evolved – it would have been overtaken by others and fallen off the radar. Take this approach with your teaching and early years setting; think about your environment, your ethos and curriculum, the children and your own practice. It is natural that something that worked three years ago no longer does now – nothing stays the same forever, and change can be positive.

Try this method and jot down some ideas in relation to your teaching methods:

- Step 1: What is working now?

- Step 2: What could work better?

- Step 3: How can I improve?

- Step 4: What do I need in order to improve?

- Step 5: How do I feel about my self-reflection?

This is a useful starting point when you self-reflect. It is important to document these changes and thoughts because the next time you do it you can reflect back once again and see the progress you have made. Perhaps you feel daunted and worried about the changes you have identified that need to take place, but once you have made them you can self-reflect and perhaps see that you didn't need to worry after all. Once again, this method of self-reflection links strongly to resilience and growth mindset – having the courage to try out new ideas, persevere when something is not going to plan and also be critical and make mistakes in order to improve.

Throughout my career in early years I have taken on various roles, all of which required me to self-reflect. As a nursery manager, I dedicated time at the end of each day to reflect, often in the car journey home or while on a walk, and I found it helped me to relive my day and work out what went well and what could have gone better, making a mental note each time I did this. Every day is a new day and we can achieve more than the day before because we are continuously learning. I would also dedicate time at the end of each month to note down in a journal my reflections and ideas for improvement, so I had a working document – my reflection journal. This type of journal can be used for your personal or work life, enabling you to develop and make progress, and ensuring that you are the best educator for your children that you possibly can be.

Reflexive practice

Once you are able to reflect after something has happened and make improvements and adjustments you will be able to begin to be reflexive too. Reflexive practice happens in the moment, not afterwards, and is a skill that can take time to master. When you have greater self-awareness, your ability to assess a situation in the moment and make changes there and then is even more productive than just simply assessing it after the event.

Throughout the day in an early years setting, there is ample opportunity to be reflexive. Let me give you a scenario…

You have planned to read *We're Going on a Bear Hunt* (Rosen and Oxenbury 1989) with a small group of children and use props to re-enact the story as you go along. You go through your expectations of the children during the activity and begin reading, but you notice that all the children are finding it hard to sit still and maintain their focus. Rather than continue, you realize that this is not quite working so you change your approach and take the children outside to get them moving. This works, as the children clearly needed to be active in order to focus, so they begin to act out the story with you in the garden area. One child begins to run around and is distracted by what else is happening in the garden, so you change your approach once again and invite that child to hold the book for you, which helps to regain their attention.

This is just one short example of the educator being fully present in the situation and picking up on the cues of the children to change and moderate their plans and approach. This reflexive practice becomes much easier when we understand our children's multiple intelligences and how they learn, because we can then adapt to their needs and style of learning, remembering that one size does not fit all when it comes to learning and development.

It is also important to note that we can become predisposed to think in a certain way, depending on our own childhood experiences and the style our parents used. Using self-reflection can make us notice these biases. Do you ever catch yourself thinking, 'Wow, I sound just like my mother/father by saying that'? I have worked with many people who were told as a child to 'stop crying and acting like a baby' when in fact now we understand that children need to show their emotion and feelings, and repressing it makes matters far worse. We know so much more and today about education, development and learning and by reflecting we can learn even more.

Helping children to reflect

Reflection is an important part of growing and developing so we should begin to instil this in children from a young age. The most productive way to do this is to take time after an activity or at the end of the day to discuss everything that happened during that period of time.

When I deliver Forest School sessions, I always make time at the end for reflection and this can take several forms:

- *Discussion:* Invite the children to sit together and take it in turns to voice what they liked and didn't like about their day. It is interesting to hear what each child remembers; usually, the children all remember different aspects and this can trigger memories for the others. Children also have the opportunity to take turns, share, communicate and listen to each other's viewpoints, which are important skills to learn. As the educator, you can then further the learning by asking questions like 'Can you tell me why you enjoyed building a den?' and 'How has today made you feel?'

- *Art:* I love to do reflection sessions around art work. This could be drawing or painting a picture, or even creating a piece of natural art on the ground to show what it was that the children enjoyed that day, or perhaps how they felt during the day. Children often find it easier to express themselves in an art form than verbally, and this is a great way to help them self-reflect.

- *Storytelling:* In a group, invite the children to relive the events of the day in chronological order to see if they can remember all that happened and tell the story of their day. You can also use reflection when you read story books to your children, encouraging them to recall the events of the story and asking them questions to further their knowledge: 'What did the troll say when then first Billy goat went over his bridge?' 'How do you think the Billy goat felt?'

- *Emotion stations:* Place visual emotion cards on the ground and ask the children to stand next to the emotion that represents how they feel about their day. Then ask the children to share why they felt this emotion. You can repeat this more than once so that they can explain all of the emotions they felt throughout the day.

It is crucial as the adult to support children to understand how to find solutions to any problems they may have had during the day, and reflection time offers this opportunity. Here is another scenario for you...

Lily and Joe were playing together in the role-play area at nursery, feeding the dolls and cooking in the role-play kitchen. Joe wanted the doll that Lily was using so he snatched the doll from her and when Lily shouted 'No!', Joe ran off with the doll. Lily began crying and Joe carried on playing.

In that moment, it is crucial for the adult to intervene to comfort Lily and help Joe to understand that his behaviour was not kind, and what he could do differently next time. Joe made a mistake and he acted on impulse based on the emotion of jealousy because he wanted the doll Lily had. Joe did not think about Lily's feelings, nor did he communicate with her, which is completely normal behaviour for a young child! Joe needs his teacher or significant adult to help him to learn and understand new strategies so when he is faced with this situation again he knows how to act. Joe is not going to master this straightaway and it will take plenty more mistakes for him to understand and learn but each time it happens he will make progress as long as an adult supports him through reflection and discussion.

Never underestimate your role as an educator. Children look to us as role models and will mirror what we say and do, so self-reflection should be a crucial part of our everyday practice both at work and personally. We become better educators and people when we have the skills to reflect and be more aware of what we are doing. Always ask yourself, what is the impact for the children if I do this? Is it a negative or positive impact? Say to yourself:

- 'If I can support a child to self-reflect on their actions, it will impact their learning because they have the opportunity to grow, learn and understand more, helping them to be emotionally intelligent.'

- 'If I am anxious and stressed when I get to work, it will impact on the children because they will pick up on my negative emotions. It will cause them to feel on edge and therefore not be relaxed to learn and play.'

Reflection supports growth mindset and resilience as it is the opportunity to assess, review and progress both for children and educators. My advice is to never become complacent! We should always strive to improve, evaluate and move forwards, the world is forever changing and evolving so we must be too.

Reflection

Self-reflection

1. Think of a time when something you were doing was not working out how you had hoped. How did you change it? What did you do?

2. Think of a time when you accomplished a task with great success. How did you do it? What method did you use?

3. Think about two positive things that have happened in the last week, and two negative. How did you manage these situations? What could you have done better or what did you learn?

Teaching reflection

1. Reflect on a time when a strategy or method supported one child, but did not work for another. What happened during and afterwards?

2. Think about a time when your mood has affected your teaching, both positively and negatively. What was the impact?

3. How do you support your children to recall events and consolidate what they have learned?

4. What is the impact of giving children the opportunity to reflect and voice themselves? How can or does this impact on your teaching?

CHAPTER 6

Moving Forwards

Now that you are a reflective educator who can support children to be resilient learners through their emotional intelligence, and you understand that all children learn differently and have unique strengths and weaknesses, you are going to build confident young children who are ready for their next stage of learning and development!

All of the chapters in this book connect with each other, both for you as the educator and for the children too. Forest School is a wonderful ethos that can create the enabling environment that supports confidence building, growth mindset, self-reflection and discovery; it also allows all types of learner the opportunity to shine.

By using the multiple intelligence approach, we can really understand and appreciate our children for the unique and wonderful individuals that they are. We can celebrate their strengths and identify their weaknesses but know that those weaknesses will not define them or make them feel inferior. We will enable them to appreciate their talents and use them to their advantage. This approach also helps you to understand yourself and your talents, and realize your worth.

By engaging with our emotions and having more self-awareness we are able to support children in understanding their emotions too. Emotional intelligence encourages positive self-awareness and regulation as well as the ability to communicate and interact with others because you can understand their emotional cues. Reflection also enables self-discovery and the development of our talents and intelligences, as well as the ability to move forwards and make improvements and progress in our lives.

Once you have finished this book, take some time to digest it first and reflect on how it links to you and your work. Then revisit it and spend some time looking into the different multiple intelligences and how they may fit in with the children you teach and care for, so that you can understand where their strengths and weaknesses lie and what types of learner they are. Next I would use the self-reflection tool and use the method on your working environment and personal life, to obtain a broad overview of how to improve and develop. Create plans and start a reflective journal to document all of your progress and achievements. This is when you can then implement the tools to support confidence, resilience and emotional intelligence in all of your children!

Before I leave you on your journey, there are a few more points that I want to make…

1. Never let anybody tell you that you cannot achieve something. There is a place in this world for everyone and their ideas. There are millions of coffee shops over the world but if you have a new idea and bring something different to the table then your coffee shop certainly has a place too, so don't be put off

by competition – the only person you should be in competition with is you, to be a better version of you.

When I was doing my A-levels, I decided to study English literature because in my GCSEs I received an 'A' grade. A few weeks into the course it was apparent that A-level English was much, much harder than the GCSE. I struggled with understanding the poetry and literature books we were studying, and it was highly embarrassing when my teacher (strongly) advised me to drop the subject, after I got a 'D' grade in my mock exams. I dropped the subject and it did leave a slight dent in my confidence. If you told me then that ten years later I would be writing my first book, I would have never believed you, but anything is possible if you are passionate and believe in yourself!

2. Children need positive role models in their lives to learn from, and you have the ability to have a lasting impact on their lives. You can help to shape their future through the opportunities that you offer for them to develop and grow. Help them to see their potential and show that you believe in them, as it will boost their confidence and self-esteem so much that they will be more receptive to learning and not giving up.

3. Childhood is not a race, nor a competition. Children learn at their own pace; we need to support and nurture their unique qualities, and be alert to their individual needs. Those children who are disadvantaged need our support even more and to have access to rich opportunities and experiences that they might not otherwise receive. There is no greater satisfaction in

my mind than watching a child flourish and succeed, knowing that you had an impact and made a difference to their lives.

4. Everyone is different and our biggest selling point is our uniqueness because there really is nobody else like you. Give yourself and your children the platform to showcase who they are and not be afraid to be themselves.

5. Balance is key. Finding balance within our everyday lives can be tricky but we need to find a happy medium that works for ourselves and the children we teach. For example, Forest School and outdoor education has its place but so does technology – find that equal balance of experiences and opportunities.

In order to continue on with your journey as an early years educator, take on board all of the chapters in this book and allow these methods and ideas to strengthen your teaching, empower your children and be the educator who inspired them.

Finally, I hope that this book has helped you on a personal level too. Please know that you are capable of anything you put your mind to and so are the children you teach – they just need the right conditions in order to blossom. And as Walt Disney once said, 'All our dreams can come true, if we have the courage to pursue them' (Hutchens 2013, p.24). I hope you find or have found your courage and that you pass it on to your children through your teaching.

Appendix: Holistic Outdoor Activity Plans

The following activity plans aim to support children's 'whole' development. They encompass all areas of learning and have been specifically created to build children's confidence, resilience and emotional intelligence.

At the end of each activity there is a reflection activity, which is extremely important in supporting the children to connect, consolidate and evaluate their learning experiences.

Please use these activity examples as a guide and build on them to create plans that suit your children, their interests and needs. Remember, there is no right or wrong way to plan activities, so use your professional judgement and try out a few ideas and methods!

ACTIVITY 1: Friendship

Activity aims:

- To support children to play and learn together collaboratively, and encourage their social confidence, self-confidence and awareness.

- To enable children to explore the outdoor environment and use its resources to create rich and meaningful play.

- To encourage discussion around the topic of 'friendship', supporting children's confidence in voicing opinions, listening to others and learning how to take turns.

Main activity:

- Set up an outdoor 'Friendship Cafe' using natural resources such as tree stumps and logs (or suitable resources you have to hand). The children design and build their cafe together.

- Create a menu of different dishes to serve! Dirt and worm pie, leaf soup and mud cupcakes are always firm favourites...

- Invite the children to take turns at role-playing the different roles needed in the cafe: waiters, chefs, customers and so on.

- Allow their play to be fluid and support their learning where necessary.

Extension:

- Support children's mathematical skills by creating a woodland currency for the cafe – stones can act as coins – to encourage the children to count and price their food and drinks.

- Support children's literacy skills by encouraging them to make marks or form letters to create the menu.

Reflection:

- Invite the children to sit together in a circle. This is a time for taking turns and sharing ideas. There are no wrong answers. First, ask the children what they enjoyed about the activity and perhaps what they didn't (don't force any child to share their views – they will do over time when they feel safe and confident enough to do so).

- Next ask the children some open-ended questions such as:

  – 'What is a friend?'

  – 'What is a good friend?'

  – 'What is a bad friend?'

  – 'How are you a friend?'

- Finally, depending on how well the children are focusing on the activity, you can read a picture book around the theme of friendship, like *Thank You For Being My Friend* by Peter Bently (2011). You may wish to read the story before you ask the friendship questions if the children are younger, as it will help to give them some relatable context.

Top tip:

- Spend a few minutes noting down your immediate observation from this activity. What went well? What didn't go so well? How would you change it in the future?

ACTIVITY 2: Who are you?

Activity aims:

- To support children to understand about themselves and others and to recognize their similarities and their differences.

- To support children to communicate with each other and have self-awareness and awareness of others, enabling respectful behaviour towards each other.

- To enable children to explore the outdoor environment and use its resources to create self-portraits.

- To encourage discussion around the topic of 'Who am I?', supporting children's confidence in voicing opinions, listening to others and learning how to take turns.

Main activity:

- Invite the children to explore the outdoor area. Take some small mirrors outside and ask the children to look at their reflections and comment on their similarities and differences.

- Encourage the children to find a space where they can create their self-portrait. This could be on the ground, on a playground or on a flat surface. Ask the children to then gather resources from the area to begin putting together a self-portrait.

- Once the children have used the natural resources to create their portraits, invite them to guess which one belongs to which child. This explores how we are all different and unique.

Extension:

- You can extend this activity by asking children to bring in photographs of their families and information about their traditions and culture to learn about each other.

Reflection:

- Invite the children to sit together in a circle. This is a time for taking turns and sharing ideas. There are no wrong answers. First, ask the children what they enjoyed about the activity and perhaps what they didn't (don't force any child to share their views – they will do over time when they feel safe and confident enough to do so).

- Next ask the children some open-ended questions such as:

  - 'What makes you, you?'

  - 'What are you good at?'

  - 'How are you different to your friends?'

  - 'Why are we all different?'

- Show the children pictures of different families from around the world so they can see how unique we all are.

Top tip:

- This can be quite a fiddly activity, especially when creating the finer details of the portrait. Children will need encouragement to do this as it will take a lot of focus and fine motor control.

ACTIVITY 3: Emotions potions

Activity aims:

- To support children to understand about their emotions and how to respond to them.

- To support children to communicate with each other and have self-awareness and awareness of others and their feelings.

- To enable children to explore the outdoor environment and use its resources to create potions.

- To encourage discussion around the topic of 'Our emotions', supporting children's confidence in voicing opinions, listening to others and learning how to take turns.

Main activity:

- Set up an outdoor 'Emotions potions' workshop using natural resources such as tree stumps and logs (or suitable resources you have to hand). The children are to design and build their workshop together.

- Using old vases and bottles from a thrift shop, invite the children to create different potions that represent the different emotions they might feel, mixing water, natural resources and some natural or food colourings (whatever you have to hand). For example, if the children are to create the emotion 'happy', ask them to relate this emotion to a colour and then mix their potion.

- When they have their different emotion potions, the children can act out with your support how they feel when they pretend to drink that emotion. This will help them to explore and consolidate each emotion.

Extension:

- Extend this activity by encouraging the children to make marks using the liquid from their potions on paper or on the ground. For example, 'Can you write a 'h' for happy?' Water-based potions are great because the children can do this on the pavement or ground and it will wash away.

Reflection:

- Invite the children to sit together in a circle. This is a time for taking turns and sharing ideas. There are no wrong answers. First, ask the children what they enjoyed about the activity and perhaps what they didn't (don't force any child to share their views – they will do over time when they feel safe and confident enough to do so).

- Next read with the children a book about emotions, like Molly Potter's (2014) *How Are You Feeling Today?* Go through each emotion and support the children to connect these emotions with a past event; discuss how it made them feel and give ideas on how to respond to that emotion in the future.

Top tip:

- Always allow the children to express themselves and give them the confidence and encouragement to voice their feelings. If they feel safe and confident that you will listen, they are more likely to share.

ACTIVITY 4: Imagination creation

Activity aims:

- To support children's imagination and curiosity through play.

- To support children to communicate with each other while playing and exploring, and to engage with their ideas and share them.

- To enable children to explore the outdoor environment and use its resources to form meaningful role-play games.

- To encourage discussion supporting children's confidence in voicing opinions, listening to others and learning how to take turns.

Main activity:

- Using a 'magical box' (this can be any box that you have or create, suitably decorated to bring a magical element to the activity), place a letter inside from a fictional character, for example, 'Sneeze the Dragon'. Sneeze the Dragon has had one of his magical eggs stolen by the woodland wizard and needs the children's help to find it! This will be your introduction to the activity, which will ignite the children's curiosity and excitement!

- Invite the children to then complete a series of tasks that will help them find the dragon's egg. There are many ways in which you can do this, some examples are:

- Have a list of items that the children have to find around the area (two sticks, four acorns, six leaves etc.). This will also support their mathematical skills.

- Ask them to search for letters hidden in the outdoor area (that you will have placed around) and once they have found them all, see if they can make the magical word (you can make this as hard or as simple as possible depending on their age).

- Create a course outside that the children have to complete, for example climbing a tree, rolling down a bank, jumping over logs (you can vary this depending on your outdoor area).

- Once the children have completed the tasks, give them a clue to where the dragon's egg can be found. Once they find the egg, encourage them to create a giant nest to protect the egg from the wizard!

- Finally, allow them to continue their own role play from this initial scenario.

Reflection:

- Invite the children to sit together in a circle. This is a time for taking turns and sharing ideas. There are no wrong answers. First, ask the children what they enjoyed about the activity and perhaps what they didn't (don't force any child to share their views – they will do over time when they feel safe and confident enough to do so).

- Next ask the children some thought-provoking questions about fictional characters, such as:

  - 'Would you rather have breakfast with a good wizard, or a bad wizard?'

  - 'If you had a magical power, what would it be?'

  - 'Are all dragons fierce?'

  - 'Are all fairies kind?'

Top tip:

- The more excited and engaged you are, the more excited and engaged the children will be! You need to enjoy activities just as much as the children! Have some fun!

References and Further Reading

References

Bently, P. (2011, first published 2008) *Thank You For Being My Friend*. Bath: Parragon Books.

Cherry, K. (2019) *5 Components of Emotional Intelligence*. Accessed on 14/09/2019 at www.verywellmind.com/components-of-emotional-intelligence-2795438

Dahl, R. (1993) *My Year*. London: Jonathan Cape.

Dempsey, E. (2010) *Recovering the Self: A Journal of Hope and Healing 11*, 1, 14.

Department for Education (2017) *Statutory frameworks for the early years foundation stage: Setting the standards for learning, development and care for children from birth to five*. Open Government Licence. Accessed on 10/07/2019 at https://assets.publishing.service.gov.uk/government/uploads/system/uploads/attachment_data/file/596629/EYFS_STATUTORY_FRAMEWORK_2017.pdf

Donaldson, J. and Scheffler, A. (1999) *The Gruffalo*. New York, NY: Dial Books for Young Reader.

Duckworth, A. (2007) 'Grit, perseverance and passion for long-term goals.' *Journal of Personality and Social Psychology 92*, 6, 1087–101.

Dweck, C. (2012) *Mindset: How You Can Fulfill Your Potential*. London: Robinson Publishers.

Dweck, C. (2016) *Mindset: The New Psychology of Success*. New York, NY: Ballantine Books.

Edutopia (2008) *Howard Gardner on Multiple Intelligences.* Interview 1997. George Lucas Educational Foundation. Accessed on 08/08/19 at www.edutopia.org/video/howard-gardner-multiple-intelligences

Gardner, H. (1993) *Multiple Intelligences.* New York, NY: Basic Books.

Hutchens, J. (2013) *The Coaching Calendar: Daily Inspiration from the 'Stress-less' Coach.* Morrisville, NC: Lulu Press, Inc.

Illeris, K. (2009) *Contemporary Theories of Learning.* Oxford: Routledge.

LitchKa, P.R. (2019) *Leading Schools with Unique Populations: An International Perspective on School Leadership.* Lanham, MD: Rowman and Littlefield.

McCloud, C. (2006) *Have You Filled a Bucket Today? A Guide to Daily Happiness for Kids.* Northville, MI: Ferne Press.

Mertz, C.J. (2010) *So, You Want To Be a Teacher.* Bloomington, IN: Xlibris.

Potter, M. (2014) *How Are You Feeling Today?* London: Bloomsbury Publishing.

Potter, M. (2018) *What's Worrying You?* London: Bloomsbury Publishing.

Rosen, M. and Oxenbury, H. (1989) *We're Going on a Bear Hunt.* London: Walker Books.

Smart, J. (2017) *Results: Think Less. Achieve More.* North Mankato, MN: Capstone.

Further reading

Armstrong, T. (2000) *In Their Own Way: Discovering and Encouraging your Child's Multiple Intelligences.* New York, NY: Penguin Putnam.

Barnes, J. V. (2020) *50 Fantastic Ideas for Forest School.* London: Bloomsbury Publishing.

Beadle, P. (2007) *Could Do Better: Help Your Kid Shine at School.* London: Transworld Publishers.

Buchan, N. (2016) *A Practical Guide to Nature-Based Practice.* London: Bloomsbury Publishing.

Cherry, K. (2019) *Gardner's Theory of Multiple Intelligences.* Very Well Mind. Accessed on 14/07/2019 at www.verywellmind.com/gardners-theory-of-multiple-intelligences-2795161

Davy, A. (2019) *A Sense of Place: Mindful Practice Outdoors.* London: Bloomsbury Publishing.

Hanscom, A. (2016) *Balanced and Barefoot: How Unrestricted Outdoor Play Makes for Strong, Confident and Capable Children.* Oakland, CA: New Harbinger.

Kelly, S. (2018) 'Empowering children with kindness.' *Parenta*, Issue 47, 10–11.

Kelly, S. (2019) 'Reflective practice vs reflexive practice.' *Parenta*, Issue 54, 32–33.

Louv, R. (2010) *Last Child in the Woods: Saving our Children from Nature-Deficit Disorder.* London: Atlantic Books.

Mayle, S. (n.d.) *Brain Development for Early Childhood Educators: Howard Gardner's Multiple Intelligences.* Harker Preschool. Accessed on 10/07/2019 at www.caisca.org/event_info/320/Brain%20Development%20for%20Early%20Childhood%20Educators%20-%20Howard%20Gardner's%20Multiple%20Intelligences.pdf

Mindset Works. *Dr Dweck's research into growth mindset changed education forever.* Accessed on 15/07/2019 at www.mindsetworks.com/science

Personality Max. *Multiple Intelligences, exploring the different types of intelligence.* Accessed on 14/07/2019 at https://personalitymax.com/multiple-intelligences

Robinson, K. (2009) *The Element: How Finding Your Passion Changes Everything.* London: Penguin Books.

Victoria, J. (2017) *Forest School & Early Years – The possibilities are endless.* Childcare Expo. Accessed on 05/05/2019 at www.childcareexpo.co.uk/forest-school-early-years-possibilities-endless-childcare-guru

Victoria, J. (2017) *Learning Through Play.* Childcare Expo. Accessed on 05/05/2019 at www.childcareexpo.co.uk/learning-play-childcare-guru

Victoria, J. (2018) 'How do your children learn best?' *Teach Early Years*, Issue 8.2, 56–57.

Victoria, J. (2018) 'Bringing fairy tales to life in a natural environment.' *Parenta*, Issue 42, 06–07.

Index

Note: page numbers given in *italics*
indicate illustrations or photographs